DK READERS

Level 2

Level 3

A Note to Parents and Teachers

DK READERS is a compelling reading programme for children, designed in conjunction with leading literacy experts, including Linda B. Gambrell, Professor of Reading at Clemson University, Clemson, S.C. Dr. Gambrell has spent many years as a teacher and teacher educator specializing in literacy development. She has served as President of the National Reading Conference, College Reading Association, and will serve as President of the International Reading Association 2007–8.

Beautiful illustrations and superb full-color photographs combine with engaging, easy-to-read stories to offer a fresh approach to each subject in the series. Each DK READER is guaranteed to capture a child's interest while developing his or her reading skills, general knowledge, and love of reading.

The five levels of DK READERS are aimed at different reading abilities, enabling you to choose the books that are exactly right for your child:

Pre-level 1 – Learning to read
Level 1 – Beginning to read
Level 2 – Beginning to read alone
Level 3 – Reading alone
Level 4 – Proficient readers

The "normal" age at which a child begins to read can be anywhere from three to eight years old, so these levels are only a general guideline.

No matter which level you select, you can be sure that you are helping your child learn to read, then read to learn!

LONDON, NEW YORK, MUNICH,
MELBOURNE, AND DELHI

For Bookwork Ltd:
Senior Art Editor Kate Mullins
Author Annabel Blackledge

For Dorling Kindersley Ltd:
Brand Manager Lisa Lanzarini
Project Editor Lindsay Kent
Publishing Manager Simon Beecroft
Category Publisher Alex Allan
Production Rochelle Talary
DTP Designer Lauren Egan

Reading Consultant
Linda B. Gambrell

First American Edition, 2005

Published in the United States by
DK Publishing, Inc.
375 Hudson Street
New York, New York 10014

05 06 07 08 09   10 9 8 7 6 5 4 3 2 1

A Cataloging-in-Publication record for this book
is available from the Library of Congress.

ISBN 0-7566-1693-X (hb.)
0-7566-1694-8 (pb.)

Reproduced by Media Development and Printing Ltd., UK
Printed and bound in China by L. Rex Printing Co. Ltd.

Discover more at
www.dk.com

Let's Go Riding

Written by Annabel Blackledge

Today is a big day for Olivia.
She is going to have
her first riding lesson.

Olivia has everything she
needs for her lesson.
She has a neat T-shirt,
a long-sleeved top, and
special riding pants
called jodhpurs (JOD-purs).
She will need to wear
a riding hat, a body protector,
gloves, and riding boots.

Safety first
Riding hats and
body protectors
are made of tough
material. They will
protect your head
and body if you fall
off a pony or horse.

When Olivia arrives
at the riding stables,
she meets three other children.
They are named Alexandra,
Holly, and Sammy.
They are waiting for
their first lesson, too.
Everyone is very excited
about learning to ride.

The children meet
their riding teacher.
Her name is Linda.
She tells them the names
of the ponies they will ride.

Linda shows the children
the large, grassy fields
and cozy stables
where the ponies live.

Then Linda shows the children
where they will have their lessons.
The sand is comfortable
for the ponies to walk on.
Olivia sees a girl on a pony.
She is learning how to jump.
"When I'm older,
I would like to do that,"
she says to Sammy.

Olivia's pony is named Honey.
Honey's coat is golden and
her mane and tail are white.

Mane

Horseshoes
Ponies wear
metal shoes on
their hooves
to protect
their feet.

Honey is a calm pony,
which is good
when you are first
learning to ride.

Mane
A pony's mane
runs from the
top of its head
to the bottom
of its neck.

Tail

Hoof

Alexandra's pony is named Mattie.
She is chestnut-colored
with a white mark on her face.
"She's so big!" says Alexandra.

Holly's pony
is named Woody.
He has beautiful
brown and white
patches and
a very soft coat.

Sammy will ride
a gray pony
named Bertie.
"Hold on tight,
Sammy!"
says Olivia.
Bertie looks
very strong!

The ponies need to be brushed every day to keep their coats glossy. Linda shows Olivia how to brush Honey's coat, mane, and tail.

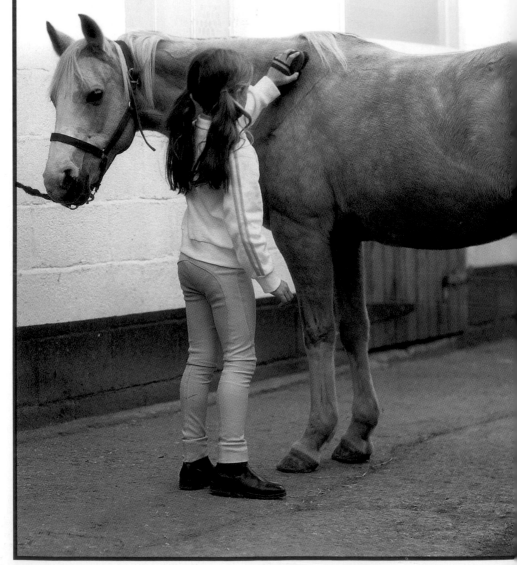

"When you brush a pony,
it's called grooming,"
Linda tells the children.

Olivia grooms Honey.
"Honey is very dirty,"
Olivia says.
"It looks like
she has been rolling
in the mud."
Honey is very relaxed
when she is groomed.

Grooming kit
A grooming kit has
all the brushes and
other equipment
that are needed
to groom a pony.

"Well done, Olivia," says Linda.
"Honey looks really nice.
Now it's time to get ready."

"First of all, we need to put
a saddle on Honey so that
you can ride her,"
explains Linda.

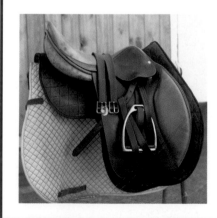

Saddle
A saddle is a leather
seat that makes
riding comfortable
and safe for the pony
and the rider.
A cloth is put on
before the saddle.

Olivia practices putting on
the saddle by herself.
She places the saddle
gently on Honey's back.
Then she fastens the straps.

Olivia's next job
is to put on Honey's bridle.

Bridle

A bridle helps a rider to control a pony. It is made up of leather straps attached to a metal bar called a bit. The bit fits inside the pony's mouth.

Olivia knows that she must be
careful and gentle with Honey.
Olivia holds the bridle
like Linda has shown her.
Then she puts the bit
into Honey's mouth and
pulls the bridle over Honey's ears.

At last, it is time
for Olivia to ride Honey.
Linda shows Olivia how to get on.
"Getting on a pony
is called mounting," Linda says.

Olivia feels nervous.
"Honey is too big,"
she says.
"I don't think
I can climb
up there."

"Yes, you can,"
says Linda.

So Olivia tries.
She puts her left foot
in the foot support
called a stirrup,
and holds on
to the saddle.

She springs up and
swings her right leg
over the saddle.
"Hooray, I did it!"
she says.

Olivia sits up straight
in the saddle and
tries to relax.

The children line up
on their ponies.
"Let's do some warm-up exercises,"
says Linda.
"They will help you learn
to trust your pony."

First the children reach back
and touch their pony's tail.

Then they reach down
and touch their toes.

Finally, they reach forward
and touch their pony's head.
"Stretch, Sammy!" calls Olivia.
"I'm trying!" Sammy laughs.

Olivia loves riding Honey.
The children ride their ponies
around and around.
Olivia feels like a real rider now.

Wild horses

Horses in the wild live in groups called herds. They eat, sleep, and move around all together.

Alexandra and Mattie lead the way. The children enjoy playing follow-the-leader.

The lesson is nearly over.
Linda asks the children
to line up on their ponies
so she can talk to them.
"I hope you enjoyed your
first riding lesson," she says.

"I liked sitting up high on Honey,"
says Olivia.
"I liked stroking Woody's soft
mane," says Holly.
"I liked everything!"
says Sammy.

"Now it's time to get off
your pony," says Linda.
"This is called dismounting."
Linda shows the children
the right way to dismount.

Olivia takes her feet
out of the stirrups.
Then she swings her leg over and
slides down to the ground.

Sammy does not want
to leave Bertie.
"Don't worry, Sammy,"
says Linda kindly.
"You can ride Bertie
again next week."

Olivia says goodbye to Honey.
She strokes her soft nose.
"Good girl, Honey," she says.
"I can't wait to ride you again.
I want to learn how to trot,
gallop, and jump!"

Fascinating facts

Horses and ponies are measured in hands. One hand is the same as 4 inches (10 centimeters). Ponies are smaller than horses.

You can tell how horses and ponies are feeling by looking at their ears. If their ears are sticking up straight and facing forward, it means that they are happy.

Horses and ponies belong to the same animal family as zebras. Their bodies are the same shape and they both have hooves and a mane. Wild zebras live in herds, like wild horses do.

Horses and ponies spend most of the time standing, but sometimes they roll around on the grass or in the mud.

Index